The Power to WIN

56 Principles to fuel and elevate your life.

T-Ray The Violinist

First Printing, 2024

Published by: T-Ray Productions, LLC
Edited and Formatted by: Williams Commerce
Cover photo by Devonte Williford of Rare Sighting Photography

Author

IG: @t_raytheviolinist
X: @trayviolinist
Facebook: T Ray The Violinist
www.traytheviolinist.com

ISBN: 979-8-9909112-0-8

Dedication

This book is dedicated to everyone who has supported me on this journey of life thus far and assisted me in finding my power to win. Thank you to my mom and dad for giving me life, grandma, extended family, and my beautiful wife, Chissel, for your daily support. I love you all dearly.

"To my beautiful daughter, Mia Ray, you have truly been a blessing to me, your Mom and the world. You have shown me first hand what it truly means to have the Power To WIN. I love you dearly and pray to be an example for you in this world!"

Introduction

Throughout my journey as a full-time music teacher, then later transitioning into a full-time artist and entrepreneur on May 26, 2014, I often worked tirelessly to find ways to stay motivated, inspired, and maintain a positive perspective to keep forging forward. Through my exposure to and consumption of motivational videos, self-growth podcasts, and countless books on self-development, I shifted my mind and perspective on life.

During this shift, I began to evolve and infuse the values I adopted from these sources into my own life and my performances on stage. In January of 2021, I returned to New Orleans, LA, from a performance in Miami, FL. While in the airport, I thought, "*How can I bring more value to my community, supporters, and the world outside the scope of my music*? At that moment, my Motivational Monday series on social media was born.

I started posting short, helpful videos addressing topics I encountered in my life. Over the past two years, I've heard stories from people I know personally and supporters of my music I met from social media expressing their thanks and gratitude for the Motivational Monday series and how they have helped them in different areas of their lives.

This book is a collection of some of the topics I've highlighted in my Motivational Monday series and a deeper dive into topics that take more time and inward work to develop. Anything we want to accomplish is truly possible, and we have all the necessary tools to make it happen within ourselves. No amount of money, external motivation, influence, or support from the outside world can change how we view ourselves. You have the power to change your life, and WE have the power to change the world through our daily decisions and perspectives. You are the artist of your life, and each day is your canvas to paint a beautiful picture to build upon the next day. You have the Power to WIN!

The Power to WIN

56 Principles to fuel and elevate your life.

How the principles work...

Each principle in this book is designed to be taken one week at a time. It is best to start with Principle 1 and work your way through to be thorough and make the best progress. However, if while skimming through this book, you find that there are principles that resonate with where you currently are in your life's journey, feel free to start there and chip away at the other principles as you see fit. This guide of principles is not meant to be a "quick fix" to solve life's problems. However, it is designed for you to progressively work towards improving many aspects of your life over time.

You will see improvement in your self-image, thinking patterns, communication skills (with yourself and others), and most of all, becoming proactive in creating the life you desire to build and live. Each principle starts with the subject and a short blurb on how each principle plays a role in your life and growth. Following each blurb will be a series of prompt questions for you to answer. It is imperative that you answer each question honestly and truthfully so that you know where you currently are. If you are unable to answer a question because you honestly don't know the answer, that is okay. However, if it is a matter of you visually seeing your truth, causing you to not want to write it down, I encourage you to push through that feeling and write it down anyway. The only way to improve is to be completely honest about where you are and where you want to be in the long run.

Exercises

Following the prompt questions will be an exercise for you to work on throughout the week. Each exercise will require daily work. Since you will only be concentrating on one principle a week, it is strongly advised to refer to the blurb, prompt questions, your answers to the questions, and the daily exercise, so you can truly internalize and actualize the steps necessary to start creating positive change.

Reflections

At the end of each week, take some time to reflect on the principal for the week and capture your reflection in the journal space provided or a separate notebook. There is no singular method or structure to writing your reflection, as your journey is your journey, and it will look different for each individual working through this book. For example, you can write about what worked well for you, the pros and cons of implementing the principle(s), how it made you feel overall, and what you are most proud of.

Each principle is designed for you to do introspective work on yourself to improve your daily lifestyle and elevate your thinking and outlook on your life to be the most successful you can be.

YOU GOT THIS!

Lastly, below are some of the exercises attached to each principle. You will see the acronym "YGT!" which stands for "You Got This!" Some exercises may be a bit more challenging than others, so this is my way of letting you know you are not alone on this journey. You have my full support, and YOU GOT THIS!

Now.... Let's Get to Work!

Peace, Love, & Strings.

-T-Ray the Violinist

Table of Contents

Principle 1

Just Start!

The first step is often the hardest step to take when we want to create positive change in our lives. We find comfort in familiarity, but some of those comforts may be holding you back and causing resistance to break free to chart your new path. However, when you take the first step, the most important thing to keep in mind when creating positive change is that you must stay consistent in your efforts and committed to improving every day.

Q: What is one thing that you have been procrastinating on and can start doing today to create positive change in your life?

A:

_____

_____

_____

Q: How can you stay committed to progressing in this area of your life?

A:

_____

_____

_____

Exercise: Think of one thing that you have wanted to start doing. Write this action step down and commit to working at it each day this week to jumpstart your progress. After you've written that down, brainstorm, and then write down how you will accomplish this.

Prompt: I want to start -

_____

_____

_____

_____

_____

_____

I will accomplish this by doing -

_____

_____

_____

_____

_____

_____

_____

Reflection

Principle 2

Keep Going!

Take it one day at a time. Not everything will go according to plan, which is a part of life's journey. The key is to remember that you must keep moving forward, adapting, and re-adjusting so that your life is in a constant flow state. Having a positive perspective and knowing you will succeed in any situation is the key to keep going!

Q: What will you do to keep a positive perspective in life when things don't go according to plan?

A:

_____

_____

_____

Q: How do you feel that shifting your perspective will keep you moving forward?

A:

_____

_____

_____

Exercise: Take a moment to think about the week you have ahead of you. What will you do to keep a positive perspective to push forward every day? Write your list of positive perspective keys below.

My positive perspective keys are:

1.

_____

_____

_____

2.

_____

_____

_____

3.

_____

_____

_____

4.

_____

_____

_____

5.

_____

_____

_____

Reflection

Principle 3

Challenges and roadblocks build character.

Challenges teach us valuable lessons about how to pivot, move forward, improve, and continue to grow in life. Adversity and roadblocks test your character and build it to learn how to adapt to different situations in life. These life lessons will equip you with tools and invaluable assets that can be used throughout the rest of your life.

Q: What is a challenge or roadblock you faced in your life? How did it make you feel, and what was your reaction?

A:

_____

_____

_____

Q: How did that experience play a role in your life and assist you in evolving to where you are now?

A:

_____

_____

_____

Exercise: The next time you encounter a challenge in life, think about the various ways that you can work through the challenge to see the other side of it.

Prompt: When presented with challenges and roadblocks in my life, I will -

_____

_____

_____

_____

_____

_____

_____

_____

_____

_____

_____

_____

_____

_____

_____

Reflection

Principle 4

Rest, Relaxation, and Rejuvenation

Rest is essential to living, leading, and optimizing our lives to create success. Relaxation and self-care are key to staying motivated, engaged, and grateful on the journey of life. When you don't properly rest and relax, you create a breeding ground for stress, anxiety, and worry to creep into your mental and physical space. Take care of your physical and mental well-being.

Q: When was the last time you unplugged to rest and relax?
A:

_____

_____

Q: How would rest, relaxation, and rejuvenation look for you moving forward?
A:

_____

_____

Q: What are the warning signs that come up for you when you need to take a break to recharge?

A:

_____

_____

Exercise: Look at your calendar and find a day in the next 30 days when you can unplug and rest.

Prompt: I will relax by -

_____

_____

_____

_____

_____

_____

_____

When I start to feel stressed in my life, I will -

_____

_____

_____

_____

_____

_____

Reflection

_____

_____

_____

_____

_____

_____

_____

_____

_____

_____

_____

_____

_____

_____

_____

_____

Principle 5

Consistency Wins

Success is created through preparation, consistent and persistent efforts, and action. No matter what you are working to accomplish in your life, it is required that you are consistent to create an environment that is conducive to winning. During the moments of hardship when you feel things don't seem to progress, remember that you may only be one step away from your breakthrough. Stay the course!

Q: What areas of your life have you been consistent in?

A:

_____

_____

Q: What areas of your life do you desire to create more consistency in?

A:

_____

_____

Q: How will your environment and actions reflect the desire to be consistent?

A:

_____

_____

Exercise: Write down one action step you can take every day for the next week to create consistency in achieving your newest goal.

Prompt: I will stay consistent in achieving my goal by -

_____

_____

_____

_____

_____

_____

_____

_____

_____

_____

_____

_____

_____

_____

_____

_____

_____

_____

Reflection

Principle 6

Actions SPEAK louder than words.

As humans, it is convenient to talk about what we want to do without taking the necessary steps to actualize what we desire in this life. The instant gratification that comes from speaking about what you want to do can feel good at the moment, but is also fleeting. It is essential to do the work rather than to speak about something that doesn't yet exist. Remember, our actions are more important and carry more value than what we say.

Q: What is an action that you would like to take in your life to manifest a dream that you have?

A:

_____

_____

_____

Q: What action steps can you execute consistently and daily to make it happen?

A:

_____

_____

_____

Exercise: Every morning as you start your day, practice reciting the following affirmation to yourself:

"I will let my actions speak louder than my words, be present, confident, and diligent in my actions to create the life I desire."

_____

_____

_____

_____

_____

_____

_____

_____

_____

_____

_____

_____

_____

_____

_____

NOTE: This powerful affirmation will set you up to have the most amazing day and proactively take action toward achieving your goals.

Reflection

_____

_____

_____

_____

_____

_____

_____

_____

_____

_____

_____

_____

_____

_____

_____

_____

_____

Principle 7

Replace trying with DOING!

The language and self-talk you use have the power to shift your perspective. "Trying" is acting with the intent that it may not work out favorably. However, "doing" and "working towards" are acting with the intention not only to execute but also to gain something from the experience and reach a target goal/destination. It is never a failed attempt (or a failure). It is a learned experience. #positiveperspective

Q: When was a time you downplayed what you were doing and used the term, "I'm trying?"

A:

_____

_____

_____

Q: How can you change the narrative of your self-talk language to manifest the "doing" aspect in your life?

A:

_____

_____

_____

Exercise: The next time you are having a conversation with someone where you are speaking about what you are currently working on, be sure to say, "I am doing _____" not, "I am trying to _____."

_____

_____

_____

_____

_____

_____

_____

_____

_____

_____

_____

_____

_____

_____

_____

_____

_____

_____

Reflection

Principle 8

Today's investment will yield tomorrow's return.

Your life investments return to you in many different shapes and forms. Your work today determines how you will prepare and show up tomorrow and beyond. Building your life one brick at a time is essential to create the house of your dreams (aka YOUR LIFE!). Focus solely on the work today, and know you'll exponentially receive your returns and dividends!

Q: What investment do you plan to make today for your future?

A:

_____

_____

_____

Q: How do you desire to see the return on that investment come into your life?

A:

_____

_____

_____

Exercise: Practice shifting your mindset in knowing that the work you are doing in your life will continue to build a strong foundation and wealth for your future!

Prompt: I will make an investment in my future today by -

_____

_____

_____

_____

_____

_____

_____

_____

_____

_____

_____

_____

_____

_____

_____

_____

_____

Reflection

Principle 9

Meet people where they are, not where you want them to be.

We all have ideas of how we would like people to show up in our lives, but the reality is that everyone is different and will approach life (and situations) in their own way. To alleviate stress, anxiety, and frustration in your life and relationships, you MUST meet people right where they are. This principle applies to family, friends, co-workers, associates, etc. Implementing this principle will assist you in properly managing your emotions and expectations of people.

Q: When was the last time you met someone where they were and didn't try to change them?

A:

_____

_____

_____

Q: In meeting them where they are, how do you process your feelings and emotions to manifest the most positive outcome?

A:

_____

_____

_____

Exercise: The next time you enter a situation or conversation with a person who you have a certain expectation of, have an open mind about how they may respond. Once they respond, take a moment to process your thoughts and then present your response.

_____

_____

_____

_____

_____

_____

_____

_____

_____

_____

_____

_____

_____

_____

_____

YGT! This may be difficult to do the first time (speaking from my own experiences). However, keep in mind that the goal is to create a relationship and conversation where expectations are established from the beginning.

Reflection

Principle 10

The only way to win is to be IN the game.

If you've watched any major sports game, you know that there are the players in the game, and then there are the players of each team on the sidelines, watching the game happen in real-time. The same applies to life. If you're in the game, you're taking action to create the life you desire. If you procrastinate by just looking at everyone around you move or overanalyzing the situation more than you are taking action, it's time to change that narrative. Get active, be PRO-ACTIVE, and get IN...THE...GAME!!!

Q: When was a time that you sat on the sidelines of life when you should've been in the game?

A:

_____

_____

_____

Q: What does it look like for you to be in the game of life going after your goals?

A:

_____

_____

_____

Q: What are some action steps that you can take right now to get in the game?

A:

_____

_____

Exercise: As you embark on your next major goal, think about some of the components you will need to take action on and create a schedule of those steps to give yourself a head start to hit the ground running.

Prompt: I will get in the game of achieving my goals by -

_____

_____

_____

_____

I will schedule time this week to do the following to reach my goal:

1.

_____

_____

2.

_____

_____

3.

_____

_____

Reflection

_____

_____

_____

_____

_____

_____

_____

_____

_____

_____

_____

_____

_____

_____

_____

_____

_____

Principle 11

Go where you are celebrated, not tolerated.

Say it louder for the people in the back! We often expend our time and energy seeking the validation of others to feel good about ourselves and to experience a sense of worthiness in the world. Unfortunately, this can lead to "social burnout" and feelings of worthlessness. Instead of concentrating on working to receive the praise of those who have no interest, seek out those who embrace and celebrate you. The term "Quality over Quantity" can't be stressed enough in this case.

Q: Have you ever been in a situation or relationship (whether plutonic or romantic) where you were tolerated instead of celebrated?

A:

_____

_____

_____

_____

Q: How can you shift the narrative and find those who celebrate you?

A:

_____

_____

_____

_____

Exercise: Take a moment to think about your personal and professional relationships, and how your interactions with people have been over time. Are there any trends or concerns that come up? If so, write those down and ask yourself, "Am I valued and appreciated in this relationship?"

YGT! If there are relationships where you question if you are valued, consider having a conversation with that person to make sure that you all are on the same page.

Prompt: I desire for the relationships in my life to look like -

_____

_____

_____

_____

_____

_____

I desire to create these types of relationships in my life -

_____

_____

_____

_____

_____

_____

Reflection

Principle 12

Get rid of the F.E.A.R. in your life.

Fear is just False Evidence Appearing Real. There is absolutely no reason to fear what you are working to accomplish in your life or an outcome that has yet to happen. Will you be perfect? No. Will you succeed 100% of the time? Yes, because there is something to be learned in every situation. Do not allow fear to rule your life or deter you from pursuing what you desire to manifest and the experiences you wish to enjoy.

Q: When was a time that you let fear guide your decisions or prevent you from doing something?

A:

_____

_____

_____

_____

_____

Q: How can you eradicate fear the next time it arises?

A:

_____

_____

_____

_____

_____

Exercise: The next time you feel fear coming up, take a moment to breathe and remind yourself that you have nothing to fear and that everything will work out in your favor. #PositivePerspective

Prompt: I will not allow fear to stop me from -

_____

_____

_____

_____

_____

_____

_____

_____

_____

_____

_____

_____

_____

_____

_____

_____

_____

Reflection

_____

_____

_____

_____

_____

_____

_____

_____

_____

_____

_____

_____

_____

_____

_____

_____

Principle 13

Your mindset is the difference between success and "failure."

You can choose to look at any situation in your life as a success or a failure. The perception of success or failure starts with your mindset. Successes speak for themselves. A failure is only a failure when you quit or adopt a negative perspective of a situation. When you take the power of shifting your perspective from negative to positive, you can see the lesson learned and the value to be taken away from the situation as opposed to looking at it as a dead end or failure.

Q: What was an experience you had in your life when you felt a sense of success and failure?

A:

_____

_____

_____

Q: In the future, how would you approach a situation that sways in the direction opposite of success to learn and grow as a person?

A:

_____

_____

_____

Exercise: This week, write down one success you had each day. It can be as big or as small as you like. However, write them down, acknowledge, and celebrate them.

Success:

1.

_____

_____

2.

_____

_____

3.

_____

_____

4.

_____

_____

5.

_____

_____

6.

_____

_____

7.

_____

_____

Reflection

Principle 14

Make room for updates!

Our lives are like computers. They must be periodically updated to run at their optimum potential. It is human nature to hang on to old habits and materials (whether physical or mental) that slow us down and prevent us from working and growing to our full potential. With self-awareness, you have the power and capabilities to eradicate those old habits and make room for fresh, new-life operating systems. It is imperative that you make updates (upgrades) to your life in every facet. Just like a computer from the year 2000, "may" (and that's a strong "may") still work, but it won't work as efficiently nor effectively as a computer that has evolved to the standards of present-day technology. You must approach your life in that same manner. Evolution and making room for updates is the key to success!

Q: What are some old files in your life that you've been holding on to that have slowed down or hindered your progress?

A:

_____

_____

Q: How can you eliminate those old files and update your life operating system? What would that look like?

A:

_____

Exercise: Write down 3 action steps you can take this week to make room for upgrades and updates in your life. As you complete each action step, write down your reason for making room in each area of your life and what your process for doing so was.

Prompt:

I will let go of -

_____
_____
_____
_____.

Action steps to upgrade and update my life:

1.

_____
_____

2.

_____
_____

3.

_____
_____

Reflection

Principle 15

Excuses prevent success.

"Paging Dr. Procrastination and Nurse Excuses." We have all made excuses as to why we "couldn't" do something or why we must "wait." Those excuses are just us psyching ourselves out to justify why we must wait or can't act on a given task. Making these excuses creates a barrier between you and creating success in your life. Ultimately, the very thing that you are running away from is the very thing that will create and cultivate the success that you desire. Don't run from taking action. That is where growth happens.

Q: When was a time you made an excuse about not doing something that would have yielded success?

A:

_____

_____

_____

_____

_____

_____

_____

_____

Exercise: Think about a task you can do today that will put you on the path to succeed at a goal you want to achieve. Write that action step down and work on it for 5-10 minutes a day this week. #ProgressOverPerfection

Prompt:

Today I will take this action to achieve my goal -

_____

_____

_____

_____

_____

_____

I will no longer make excuses in my life about -

_____

_____

_____

_____

_____

_____

Reflection

Principle 16

Get 1% better every day.

It is easy for us to create grandiose benchmarks and goals each day (I'm super guilty of this.) When we create a list of goals and benchmarks, it can look like a seemingly impossible mountain to climb all at once, and we reach the end of the day feeling as though we didn't accomplish anything because we didn't complete everything on our to-do list. This inevitably leads to a sense of feeling unproductive. Let's dial it back and plan to execute 1 or 2 major tasks a day to create incremental progress, which is the 1% better everyday principle. There are 365 days in a year, and if you work to be 1% better every day, you will yield a 365% return on your goals.

Q: When was a time that you felt overwhelmed by your goal list and felt as though progress was not being made?

A:

_____

_____

_____

Q: Moving forward, how can you reshape and approach your goals in such a way that you are able to not only see but feel a sense of accomplishment at the end of each day?

A:

_____

_____

_____

Exercise: Write down one goal for this week and create an action plan to achieve it using the 1% Better Everyday principle.

Goal:

_____

_____

_____

_____

Action steps to accomplish my goal:

1.

_____

_____

_____

_____

2.

_____

_____

_____

_____

3.

_____

_____

_____

_____

Reflection

Principle 17

Maximum effort creates MAXIMUM results!

The more time, effort, and energy we put into something, the higher the likelihood it will be returned and met with maximum results. When you give maximum effort to any part of your life, it may not return immediately. However, it will eventually return in the form (or as close to) the outcome you desire. Put in the work, and the rest will follow!

Q: When working to achieve a specific goal in your life, how do you maximize your efforts to ensure that you create the best possible outcome?

A:

_____

_____

_____

_____

_____

Q: What are some things that you can do daily to maximize your time to create the desired result?

A:

_____

_____

_____

_____

_____

Exercise: Write down 5 things that you feel are preventing you from reaching your maximum effort. Work daily this week to eliminate those 5 things with small incremental habit changes.

1.

_____

_____

2.

_____

_____

3.

_____

_____

4.

_____

_____

5.

_____

_____

Prompt:

When I put forth maximum effort in my life it looks and feels like -

_____

_____

_____

_____

_____

Reflection

Principle 18

There's more than one way to get to your destination.

When driving your vehicle to a given destination, sometimes you encounter roadblocks that come in many different shapes and forms: an accident, road closures, construction, etc. When you encounter those obstacles, nine times out of 10, you know of an alternate route or use your GPS to find an alternate route to get you to your destination. You must apply this same methodology to your life when working to reach a destination (a.k.a. your GOALS). It is easier to go down the path of least resistance or the path that worked for someone else. But keep in mind that your journey is YOUR journey, and the path to your destination will be uniquely its own. Don't give up, embrace it, and don't run from it.

Q: When met with obstacles in the pursuit of goals in your past, did you quit or find an alternate route to achieve your goal?

A:

_____

_____

Q: If you found an alternate route, what was your thought process for pivoting to still create the desired outcome of achieving your goal?

A:

_____

_____

_____

Exercise: If you find yourself at a roadblock this week whether physically, mentally, or emotionally, think about some of the ways that you can quickly redirect your energy to create the positive outcome of reaching your destination.

Prompt:

When I encounter a roadblock, I will do this to overcome and reach my goals -

_____

_____

_____

_____

_____

_____

_____

_____

_____

_____

_____

_____

_____

Reflection

Principle 19

There is a blessing in every opportunity.

Every opportunity in your life presents you with a myriad of chances to receive a blessing (and also to BE a blessing). As humans, it is easy to focus solely on the one (or two) things we desire to attain from an opportunity. However, there's usually a host of other blessings right where you are. Be open to the fact that the one thing you desire may not come to pass at that moment, but realize that the opportunity in front of you may be a blessing in disguise. It is also important to know that you can be of service to others in a genuine way that will create opportunities.

Q: Have you had an opportunity in your life and visualized exactly how it would go in the moment and what your desired outcome would be?
A:

_____

_____

_____

Q: When the outcome didn't go according to your visualization, were you disappointed, or did you do a mental check to regroup and stay present?
A:

_____

_____

_____

Exercise: The next time you are presented with an opportunity, practice the mindfulness of being present and open to the various blessings that may come from that opportunity

Affirmation:

"I will be present and grateful for every opportunity that comes my way while being of service to others."

_____

_____

_____

_____

_____

_____

_____

_____

_____

_____

_____

_____

_____

_____

_____

_____

_____

Reflection

Principle 20

Exude DOPENESS and the rest will follow.

We live in an instant gratification world where the majority of society wants it quick, fast, and in a hurry. When posting a picture or video on social media, we chase the dopamine high of people liking, sharing, commenting, and giving praise. However, when the desired outcome doesn't happen, we can feel unacknowledged, invisible, and inadequate. This principle applies online and in real life, in real-time. The focus of your efforts and work should be on the craft of what you are doing. Staying engaged in the process and putting your best foot forward is the ultimate high. As the saying goes, build it, and they will come. Create your DOPENESS, and they will come!

Q: Do you focus on the product of your craft more than the reaction (instant gratification) that others will give you when you put it out into the world?

A:

_____

_____

Q: If you find yourself focusing on the reaction of others more than the product, what are some modifications you can make to your mindset to focus on the craft of your work?

A:

_____

_____

_____

Exercise: This week focus your energy toward putting work into the project that you are currently working on. Whether it's a project for work, a book you are writing, painting, music project, etc. Create the time and environment this week to focus solely on making progress on that specific thing.

Affirmation:

"I will focus on my craft and trust the process and work I am currently engaged in."

_____

_____

_____

_____

_____

Prompt:

When I create my DOPENESS it looks like -

_____

_____

_____

_____

_____

_____

_____

_____

_____

Reflection

Principle 21

You can't play small and win BIG!

To win big, your efforts must match what is required to yield big results (refer to Principle 17: Maximum efforts create maximum results). For example, if you desire to be a world-renowned painter, you must make major investments in yourself and your business to create opportunities to build your brand outside your comfort zone. You can't only paint in your gallery and expect the world to come to you and put your work out into the world (I am not saying this can't happen if the right person walks in. However, that is quite an anomaly). We must create the ideal environment to cultivate the BIG wins! For example, save money to plan a trip to connect with artists in various cities around the country and find out if a big art festival is happening in a foreign country that will give you the opportunity to put your work in front of an international audience. There are so many ways to expand beyond your wildest imagination. Again, these investments may not yield a return right away. However, when you plant the seed of intention, the world has no choice but to conform to you.

PLAY BIG, WIN BIG!

Q: Is there a time that you played small and expected a big win?

A:

_____

_____

_____

Q: If so, what is your thought process behind playing small and staying in your comfort zone? Fear of judgment or failure?

A:

_____

_____

_____

Exercise: Think of a goal that you want to accomplish that will take large-scale planning, effort, time, and capital to accomplish. Create a roadmap and plan to accomplish that goal.

YGT! This may be scary but take a deep breath, visualize yourself in that moment and take action! It will all work out in your favor!)

Goal:

_____

_____

_____

Action steps to achieve my goal:

1.

_____

_____

2.

_____

_____

3.

_____

_____

—

Reflection

Principle 22

Remember why you started.

How we start and how we finish can look totally different. Take a moment to close your eyes and visualize where you were and how you felt when you started your career, a new job, or a relationship. Now, fast-forward through time and take note of the various things that have happened since that moment up until the present day. Do you feel the same or different? (Whether more excited or on autopilot)

Now, think about why you started your career, job, or relationship. Keep that visual in your mind and take note of that every morning when you wake up.

The purpose of this is to put things back into perspective to remember why you started. In some cases, you may be far away from your reason and have lost your interest or passion, and that is okay. This just means that it is time to look within to figure out which direction you should go from here. In other cases, your why may have evolved beyond your initial reasoning for starting, and that is great! This means that you have grown and have found a deeper purpose and meaning to the work that you are doing.

Q: If you have lost your spark, what is something that you feel you can do to regain it in your "why"?

A:

_____

_____

_____

_____

_____

Q: If the spark is gone for good, where do you see yourself transitioning in life to regain an excitement in your "why?"

A:

_____

_____

_____

Exercise: Write down what your why is in the space below. If your "why" has evolved, list the ways that you feel you have grown and what your deeper purpose is within the work that you are doing.

My Why:

_____

_____

_____

_____

_____

My evolution & growth:

1.

_____

_____

2.

_____

_____

3.

_____

_____

Reflection

Principle 23

Have fun!

As adults, over time, we seem to lose a lot of our luster for the fun things in life for various reasons, such as jobs, family life, financial obligations (or financial stress), etc. We get caught up in the rat race of life and start to feel as though fun expires after a certain age (I'm guilty of this). Truthfully, fun is what assists us in maintaining a youthful spirit and continuing to have a desire for life outside of our day-to-day tasks and obligations. It is essential that you find fun and joy in your life to have a sense of fulfillment.

Q: When was the last time you had fun in your life?

A:

_____

_____

_____

_____

Q: What can you do to maintain fun in your life or reinvigorate it if it has been lacking?

A:

_____

_____

_____

_____

Exercise: Take a few moments this week to remember some of the things you used to do that brought you joy and were fun. Figure out how you can incorporate some of those activities back into your schedule (even if it's only once a month).

YGT! We must balance our lives out so that we can truly enjoy all aspects of our lives.

Things that bring me joy:

1.

_____

_____

2.

_____

_____

3.

_____

_____

Prompt

When I experience fun and joy, it looks like -

_____

_____

_____

_____

_____

_____

Reflection

Principle 24

If you don't make the SHIFT, then you'll never make the CHANGE!

Changing out of our old ways can be very uncomfortable. However, if we want different results in our lives, then we must do things differently. There may be a shift and change that you desire to make in your life, but something is holding you back. Think about what those things are. Is it waiting to move to a new city with more opportunities to grow? Perhaps changing career fields to something that brings you more fulfillment? Or elevating your current business to create more revenue and support? Shift your efforts and CHANGE YOUR LIFE!

Q: What is something you continued to do that yielded the same results over and over?

A:

_____

_____

Q: What do you feel is preventing you from shifting out of this old way of operating into a fresh, new way?

A:

_____

_____

Exercise: Make a list of things you want to shift in your life and change. Once you have your list, create an action plan as to how you will make these various changes and shift your life.

I want to change the following aspects of my life:

1.

_____

2.

_____

3.

_____

Action steps and plan

_____

_____

_____

G (Goal) + P (Plan) + AS (Action Steps) = C (CHANGE)

_____

_____

_____

NOTE: Insert boxes here for G+P+AS = C

Reflection

Principle 25

Take it one day at a time.

Yesterday is gone, and tomorrow isn't here yet; all you have is today and this present moment. Your mindset plays a major role in taking it one day at a time. There is only so much that can be accomplished in one day, and you must focus your energy on today. Yes, plan for tomorrow and the foreseeable future, but you must stay engaged and present with the gift of today. Build your life one day at a time. #BrickbyBrick

Q: In your life thus far, do you feel like you have kept the perspective of taking things one day at a time or find yourself desiring to rush to the end of the process to reach your goal?

A:

_____

_____

Q: If you have "rushed" through the process to reach your goal, what was the reasoning? How did you feel in the process? Hurried, frustrated, anxious? Take some time to elaborate on this.

A:

_____

_____

Exercise: Practice mindfulness today. Think about what you want to accomplish today (and only today) and write that list of things down, prioritizing the most important things first. Be open to achieving each of those goals and embracing the process of achieving them (some may take longer than others). Repeat this exercise each day this week.

YGT! If you don't achieve everything on your list for today, give yourself grace and be open to rolling those items over to your list for the next day. Remember, there will always be things on your "to-do" list, so work diligently and gracefully.

Today's Goals:

1.

_____

_____

_____

_____

2.

_____

_____

_____

_____

3.

_____

_____

_____

_____

Reflection

Principle 26

Find joy and gratitude in every situation.

Having an attitude of gratitude is key to living a fulfilled and successful life. When you feel and express your gratitude, you are more likely to exhibit joy and internal peace. Not everything will go according to plan or how you expect it to go. However, in every situation you encounter, there will be a moment where you can feel joy and express gratitude. Have an attitude of gratitude.

Q: Is there a moment recently in your life when you found it hard to express joy and gratitude?

A:

_____

_____

_____

_____

_____

Q: Moving forward, how can you feel joy and express your gratitude in your life?

A:

_____

_____

Exercise: Each day this week, write down 5 things you are grateful for that happened that day. Once you have taken time to write these 5 things down, take some time to reflect on why you are grateful for them.

I am grateful for:

1.

_____

_____

_____

2.

_____

_____

_____

3.

_____

_____

_____

4.

_____

_____

_____

5.

_____

_____

_____

Reflection

Principle 27

Where there's a WILL there's a WAY
to reach your destination.

Willpower is the one human superpower that we all possess. Whether you know it or not, you have the mental fortitude to will yourself to do phenomenal things in your life. When you encounter obstacles on your journey to achieve something great, it is only a test of your willpower to push through to the finish line. Let your willpower work for you, not against you!

Q: Have you ever experienced a time when you had to will yourself to push through a difficult or challenging time in your life? How did you feel as you were going through the process?

A:

_____

_____

_____

Q: What did it look like on the other side of the challenge once you reached your destination?

A:

_____

_____

Exercise: Think about a current or upcoming project/goal that you will be working to accomplish. Once you have that visual in your mind, walk yourself through every part of achieving that goal and how it will feel to use your will power to create greatness.

Mind Map

_____
_____
_____
_____
_____
_____
_____
_____

Goal

_____
_____
_____
_____
_____
_____
_____
_____

Reflection

Principle 28

People will quit on you, but don't you DARE give up on yourself!

When working to accomplish something phenomenal, you must honor the vision and never quit. The reality is that everyone won't see your vision (no matter what phase of the journey you are in), and some people will quit on you, and that is okay! Often, people won't "buy in" to what you are working to accomplish until they can see tangible results, which may take months or years to accumulate. Most importantly, you don't quit on yourself because of someone else's lack of belief in you. Become okay with the reality that there will be people who quit on you. No one (and I mean no one) will believe in you or your vision more than you!

Q: Think of a time when someone quit on you. How did that feel? What were your thoughts and how did you move past that moment?

A:

_____

_____

Q: The next time someone quits on you, how will you handle the situation to continue progress on your goal and in your life's journey?

A:

_____

_____

Exercise: As you move through this week, think about the commitments that you have made to others and the ones that people have made to you. Be observant of how you walk, talk, and act towards that commitment and vice versa as it pertains to their commitment to you.

Prompt

1. When I make a commitment to others I will -

_____

_____

_____

_____

_____

_____

_____

_____

2. If someone quits on me in the future, I will approach the situation by doing -

_____

_____

_____

_____

_____

_____

_____

_____

Reflection

Principle 29

Know your value and worth.

Before the world can see your value and worth, you must look in the mirror and see it within yourself. We all possess greatness and have the infinite ability to bring value into this world. You must see, feel, and exude your value for others to acknowledge, respect, and embrace. Do not allow yourself to be in situations where you aren't valued, and your worth is lowballed. Stand firm in your core principles as a person and know your worth!

Q: Have you ever been in a situation where your value and worth weren't being taken seriously? Did you stay in that situation or remove yourself from it?

A:

_____

_____

Q: Moving forward, how will you clarify that you value yourself and know your worth? (This can be in a friendship, romantic relationship, workplace, business partnership, etc.)

A:

_____

_____

_____

Exercise: Write down your core values and how you expect to be treated in the various parts of your life.

Affirmation: "I am worthy, value myself, and bring value wherever I am.

_____

_____

_____

_____

Core Values:

1.

_____

_____

2.

_____

_____

3.

_____

_____

4.

_____

_____

5.

_____

_____

Reflection

Principle 30

Build compound interest in your life by investing in today's efforts.

The work we put into our lives today will directly affect our future. We may not be able to see the progress being made on the micro-scale. However, in the long-term macro, we can measure our progress in such a way that shows how the work and effort that is put in consistently over a long period of time can yield a great return. Just as when the walls of a house are being built, each brick must be meticulously laid, mortared, and set to create a strong exterior. Build your life's compound interest brick-by-brick.

Q: Is there an area of your life where you currently see the compound interest growing for your future?

A:

_____

_____

Q: What is something that you can start doing today that will slowly day-by-day create compound interest in a particular area of your life?

A:

_____

_____

_____

_____

Exercise: Write out 5 small tasks that will assist you this week in building compound interest in your life's endeavors. Once you write these five tasks down, create a schedule where you can incorporate each of them into your daily routine.

Compound Interest Task

1.

_____

_____

2.

_____

_____

3.

_____

_____

4.

_____

_____

5.

_____

_____

Sun.   Mon.   Tues.   Wed.   Thurs.   Fri.   Sat.

Reflection

Principle 31

Don't half step on actualizing what you want to manifest in your life.

We all desire to live the most magnificent, fulfilled life possible. However, there can be things in the way that prevent us from doing so. Often, fear is the driving force that makes us half-step on actualizing what we want to manifest in our lives. The fear of judgment and criticism can cause us to shrink ourselves to live a life well below our manifestation benchmark. Today, I challenge you to live fully and boldly in the life you desire to live. Don't half-step. Take full control of manifesting your destiny!

Q: Do you feel like you are half-stepping on the life you truly desire to live?

A:

_____

_____

_____

Q: What are 3 action steps you can take today to begin manifesting the life you truly desire to live?

A:

_____

_____

_____

Exercise: This week, work confidently, diligently, and consistently to create the life you desire to manifest. Write down 3 things you will do daily in each area to build your dream life.

I will confidently:

1.

_____

2.

_____

3.

_____

I will diligently work to:

1.

_____

2.

_____

3.

_____

I will consistently:

1.

_____

2.

_____

3.

_____

Reflection

Principle 32

Calculate your steps before you reach your destination.

Just as when a person is driving a car to a destination they have never been to, they must first put the GPS on to see exactly what route they must take to reach their destination. The same applies when you are working to reach goals in your life. You must first calculate how you will get there to make the necessary and proper steps to reach it. Yes, you may have to modify your steps and route along the way. However, when you take the time to prepare and calculate the work, resources, and time (if applicable), you set yourself up to have a greater chance of being successful in reaching your destination.

Exercise: As you prepare for the journey of accomplishing your next major goal, take some time to calculate what your route and strategy will look like. Brainstorm those ideas in the space provided below. Make sure to leave room in your plan to modify things if necessary.

Route:

_____

_____

_____

_____

_____

_____

_____

_____

Strategy:

_____

_____

_____

_____

_____

_____

_____

_____

_____

_____

_____

_____

Destination:

_____

_____

_____

_____

_____

_____

_____

_____

_____

_____

_____

Reflection

Principle 33

STAY FOCUSED
don't get distracted.

It can be easy to start and then have your attention diverted to things that are seemingly unrelated to your current goal(s). We constantly have obstacles being thrown at us daily by life in various forms. However, it is important to maintain focus and modify our schedules accordingly to complete the task at hand.

If you committed to doing one hour of work a day on your current project, stay focused and execute for that one hour.

Q: What is a project you worked on in the past where you continued to be distracted and didn't fully complete?

A:

_____

_____

_____

Q: How can you eliminate distractions in the future to create the most conducive environment for success? Is it putting your phone on D-N-D (Do Not Disturb) or placing it in another room during the time that you are working? Is it declining to go out this weekend or on a trip that will take away precious time from completing your project? What will work best for you to eliminate distractions?

A:

_____

_____

_____

Exercise: Write down what distractions you're currently allowing into your life that are hindering you from completing your current goals and tasks. Next, create a plan on how to minimize those distractions as you work throughout the week.

My current distractions are:

1.

_____

_____

2.

_____

_____

3.

_____

_____

I will minimize my distractions by:

1.

_____

_____

2.

_____

_____

3.

_____

_____

Reflection

Principle 34

Self-doubt is the killer of dreams.

If we don't believe in ourselves, then who else will? Self-doubt is the biggest killer of dreams and living life to its full potential. We've all dealt with moments of doubt, whether it was wondering if we were skilled enough to accomplish something or the fear of judgment from others. The truth is that when you believe 100% in your abilities and exude that confidence out into the world, YOU ARE UNSTOPPABLE! Eradicate your self-doubt and negative self-talk to make room for the unstoppable force of nature that you are meant to be!

Q: When was a moment you experienced self-doubt of your own abilities?
A:

_____

_____

_____

Q: What would it look like for you to have a positive perspective and confidence in yourself moving forward? What would you say to yourself to create a positive mindset in your environment?
A:

_____

_____

Exercise: When doubt creeps in this week, repeat the following affirmation.

Affirmation:

"I am here because I am highly qualified, capable, and possess all of the necessary knowledge to accomplish my goal."

_____
_____
_____
_____
_____
_____
_____
_____
_____
_____
_____
_____
_____
_____
_____
_____
_____
_____
_____
_

Reflection

_____

_____

_____

_____

_____

_____

_____

_____

_____

_____

_____

_____

_____

_____

_____

_____

_____

_____

_____

Principle 35

Are you about that life?!

To be phenomenal in life, we must be willing to do things that have never been done before and go places that have never been gone. When you set out to accomplish a particular goal in your life, it is at that moment that you are making a commitment and covenant to achieve greatness. Before starting each goal or transition, ask yourself, Am I really about that life? Am I really willing to do the work and make the sacrifices to reach my goal? Will I stay consistent, even when I am tired?

It is easy to get excited and "say" that you want to do something, but it is more important that you take the time to visualize yourself being engaged in the process and present doing the work to accomplish your goal. Take a few minutes to visualize yourself engaged in the work of your goal.

Q: Now that you have that visualization, can you see yourself engaging in every facet of the process to achieve your goal? If so, great! If not, what do you think needs to happen so that you can be engaged in each aspect?

A:

_____

_____

_____

_____

_____

_____

_____

_____

Exercise: For your next major goal, take some time to write what the goal is and all the things that will be required to reach that goal.

Goal:

_____

_____

_____

_____

_____

_____

Requirements for me to meet my goal:

1.

_____

_____

2.

_____

_____

3.

_____

_____

Reflection

Principle 36

Assess, Acknowledge, Execute!

Sometimes, it is difficult to understand why a certain aspect of our life isn't working out how we would like it to. Humans can easily fall into a subconscious cycle of doing things without realizing it. But you can change all of that in your life! Sometimes, all you need to do is pause to assess your current situation, acknowledge what you need to change, decide to change it, and execute! Every action has an opposite and equal reaction. You must make sure that all your actions are aligned to create an environment where you can properly execute!

Q: What is something in your life that you have been wanting to accomplish and find yourself stuck in a rut or toxic cycle that is preventing you from reaching that goal?

A:

_____

_____

_____

Q: Moving forward, what is one major shift that you can make to improve your odds of success?

A:

_____

_____

Exercise: Write out what you feel is holding you back and some of the aspects you need to address and change by using the AAE method.

Assess (What do I need to change?)

1.

_____

2.

_____

3.

_____

Acknowledge (Where I am falling short?)

1.

_____

2.

_____

3.

_____

Execute (Take action to create the change)

1.

_____

2.

_____

3.

_____

Reflection

Principle 37

The reciprocity of energy

Energy is the fuel for everything in our lives, not just physically, but mentally, through our processing system and interactions with others. If you want to attract positivity and abundance, you must exemplify that type of energy. It is the law of good karma and reciprocity for it to return to you.

Q: What type of energy are you putting out into the world? Are you doing and saying things with a positive intention?

A:

_____

_____

_____

_____

Q: How can you change your mindset to create more of the energy you desire to have in your life?

A:

_____

_____

_____

_____

Exercise: This week, think about some of the people and activities you will be engaged in. As you think through every situation, visualize setting the stage for positive thinking and a positive outcome.

Affirmation:

"I will create positive thoughts and actions as I move through each day of my life. My reality will reflect my positive thinking."

_____

_____

_____

_____

_____

_____

_____

_____

Prompt

When I have positive thoughts, I will -

_____

_____

_____

_____

_____

_____

_____

When I have negative thoughts, I will eradicate them by:

1.

_____

_____

_____

_____

_____

_____

2.

_____

_____

_____

_____

_____

_____

3.

_____

_____

_____

_____

_____

_____

Reflection

Principle 38

The terms of your life are NON-NEGOTIABLE.

This goes hand in hand with knowing your worth and value. (Principle 29). For each of us, there are certain aspects of our lives that are non-negotiable, both personally and professionally. It is essential that you set boundaries around those aspects to assist you in staying fully aligned with your core principles. When you compromise on your non-negotiables, you send a strong message to yourself and the outside world that you don't value yourself. So, it is imperative to set the stage early. Stand firm on your non-negotiables!

Q: What is a non-negotiable in your life that you have negotiated on?
A:

_____

_____

_____

_____

Q: How would it look to not negotiate on that term in your life?
A:

_____

_____

_____

Exercise: Write down five non-negotiables for your life and how you will establish those boundaries.

1.

_____

_____

_____

2.

_____

_____

_____

3.

_____

_____

_____

4.

_____

_____

_____

5.

_____

_____

_____

YGT! It is quite possible that you may be met with some resistance from people for what you have deemed non-negotiable in your life. You must understand that it is much more important to remember that your peace of mind is much more important than the outside world's reaction.

Reflection

Principle 39

Dress for success, not to impress.

Whether you work for yourself or an employer, how you dress can say a lot (or a little) about how you will perform on the job. To be clear, this doesn't mean you must dress up in a suit or dress (especially if you work in a field that is not conducive to work attire, such as a construction site). However, this does mean that one should take pride in their attire. Even if it is a simple uniform, a shirt with the company logo, and some khaki pants. Take the time to iron the shirt and pants. Even that small action can say a lot to an employer, potential client, team members, and customers. It says that "this person is serious about their work and wants to present the highest quality customer service experience possible." You never know who you will meet on your journey, so it is best to dress for success!

Q: Are you dressing for success or just dressing to get through the day?

A:

_____

_____

_____

Q: If not, what would it look like for you to dress for success?

A:

_____

_____

_____

Exercise: This week, as you are preparing for work, a meeting, or planning to attend some events (whether personal or professional events), take into consideration your wardrobe and how what you wear plays a role in how the world will receive you). Show that you are powerful, confident, and focused.

Attire for the week:

Sunday:

_____

_____

_____

Monday:

_____

_____

_____

Tuesday:

_____

_____

_____

Wednesday:

_____

_____

_____

Thursday:

_____

_____

_____

Friday:

_____

_____

_____

Saturday:

_____

_____

_____

_____

Reflection

Principle 40

Focus and go hard!

We addressed focus in Principle 34; however, magic happens when focus and intense work join forces. To be clear, this doesn't mean working for 24 hours straight or being extreme. This means you must be super vigilant in making sure that you are executing at a very high level. To achieve greatness, each of the following is essential:

1. Confidence in your abilities.
2. Focus
3. Work Ethic
4. Determination
5. Grit to go hard when it counts.

Q: Do you know when it is time for you to go hard?

A:

_____

_____

_____

_____

Q: What does "going hard" look like in your life and when you're working to achieve your goals?

A:

_____

_____

_____

_____

Exercise: Write down what your day and week will look like when you are laser-focused and intentional about the work that you are doing to achieve your goals. Also, think about how you will implement these characteristics into your daily flow.

Prompt: When I am consistent and focused, it looks and feels like:

_____

_____

_____

_____

_____

_____

_____

_____

_____

_____

Reflection

Principle 41

The more you know, the more you GROW!!

There is a wealth of knowledge in the world beyond where you currently are. It can be easy to think that if the way we operate is working, then that is as good as it can get, which couldn't be further from the truth. There is always a more effective way to think, do, and be in the world. Take the initiative to explore the world beyond where you are to expand your knowledge and view of the world. Your perspective of the world and self-image will change in ways you couldn't have imagined. Knowledge truly is power; the more you accumulate in your life, the more you will evolve and GROW!

Q: What is a "magic moment" in time where you experienced something that transformed your life and perspective in a positive, long-lasting way?

A:

_____

_____

_____

_____

Q: How can you ensure that you consistently have these moments in your life to continue to grow?

A:

_____

_____

_____

_____

Exercise: Write down three knowledge and self-growth outlets or pieces of literature you can indulge in this week to expand your mindset. This can be a book, podcast, or YouTube interview of someone you look up to in your field of work, etc. Schedule at least 15-20mins a day this week to be fully immersed in your chosen self-growth outlets and literature.

Knowledge and Self-Growth Activities:

1.

_____

_____

_____

_____

_____

2.

_____

_____

_____

_____

_____

3.

_____

_____

_____

_____

_____

Reflection

Principle 42

Be clear and concise about your goals.

Being clear and concise about your goals can be challenging when not equipped with the right mindset and focus. It is important to take some time to write down your goals and get clear about what they are, how you will accomplish them, and most importantly, why you want to accomplish them. You must also be realistic about the time and attention required to reach said goals and, more importantly, prioritize them. You may have three major goals you want to accomplish, and they all will require a massive amount of your time, so it is important to rank them from most to least important and focus on them individually. You want to set yourself up for success by not becoming overwhelmed with too many tasks and self-imposed pressure.

Q: Are you clear about your current goals in life, whether they are personal or professional?

A:

_____

_____

_____

_____

_____

_____

Q: Have you taken the time out to create a gameplan on how you will accomplish your goals and stay focused on making incremental progress each day?

A:

_____

_____

_____

_____

_____

_____

_____

Exercise: Write down one major goal you plan to accomplish this week. Once you write it down, break the goal down in even more detail.

For example:

Goal: I will write 10 new pages for my book this week.

_____

_____

_____

_____

_____

_____

_____

_____

Detailed Goal: I will work on writing 10 new pages for chapter 2 of my book as it pertains to _____ subject matter.

This week's goal:

_____
_____
_____
_____
_____
_____
_____

Goal:

_____
_____
_____
_____
_____
_____
_____

Detailed Goal:

_____
_____
_____
_____
_____

Reflection

Principle 43

Come from a place of love and gratitude.

Love and gratitude are two of the most powerful things that can help us live successful lives. When we do things from a place of love and passion, that energy will resonate and transcend beyond where we currently are. People will be attracted to your loving nature and know you are genuine with your actions and approach to any situation. Gratitude is the "secret sauce" that keeps on giving. When you show gratitude for everything (and everyone) in your life, living a fulfilled life becomes much easier. As humans, it is easy to want more and have more, but when you take a moment to exhibit thanks and gratitude for what you currently have and where you currently are, the blessings will flow even more abundantly.

Q: What are the ways that you show your gratitude both internally and externally?

A:

_____

_____

_____

_____

_____

_____

_____

Exercise: Each day this week, take a moment to express your gratitude for at least 3 things (if there are more than 3, GREAT!). Whether at the beginning or end of the day, write down your list of gratitude.

Sunday Gratitude

_____

_____

Monday Gratitude

_____

_____

Tuesday Gratitude

_____

_____

Wednesday Gratitude

_____

_____

Thursday Gratitude

_____

_____

Friday Gratitude

_____

_____

Reflection

Principle 44

Collaboration is bigger than competition.

No person succeeds on their own. Success is compounded on the foundation of support from people in our lives, and that must be acknowledged. In some industries, there is a cultural environment that unknowingly says "there can only be one" when, in fact, that isn't true. There are billions of people living on this planet, and it would be insane to think that there can only be "one" person doing one specific thing and no one else. This is where collaboration comes in and shows you that to grow and become sharper, one must be open to collaborating with others. As mentioned earlier, "the more you know, the more you grow." That mantra rings true in this principle as well. You can provide value to others and vice versa. As the saying goes, "iron sharpens iron."

Q: Do you collaborate with others to sharpen your skills and knowledge while providing value to others?

A:

_____

_____

_____

_____

Q: How would you like to see collaboration manifest in your life?

A:

_____

_____

_____

_____

Exercise: If you haven't collaborated with someone, write down the names of three people or companies in your industry that you would like to collaborate with and how you desire to collaborate with them. Take some time to find someone in your field of work that you can create a collaborative project with.

I will collaborate with:

1.

_____

_____

_____

2.

_____

_____

_____

3.

_____

_____

_____

YGT! Reaching out to people about collaborating may seem scary at first but I encourage you to put yourself out there to make it happen. Also, make sure that these collaborations are genuine, authentic, and not forced. Both you and the person(s) you are collaborating with should bring value to the table. This shouldn't be a one-sided transaction. YOU GOT THIS!

Reflection

Principle 45

Make yourself being a priority, a priority.

We often make the mistake of expecting others to make what we have going on in our lives or what we are working to accomplish a priority in their lives and schedules. The reality is that no one will make your life or goals a priority more than you will. All of us are working to accomplish something great and meaningful in the world, which often means that projects & inquiries from others will take the back burner. This doesn't warrant frustration towards the other individuals. However, this is a moment where you take a look at yourself and internalize that you must prioritize yourself and your goals. If others want to join in to contribute, great! But if they don't, you must have a plan of action to accomplish your goals regardless. If you don't make yourself a priority, then who will?

Q: Has there been a time when you depended on someone else to make your dream a priority? If so, did that person follow through on assisting you with your priority? If not, how did that situation transpire?

A:

_____

_____

_____

_____

_____

Q: What did you learn and take away from this experience?

A:

_____

_____

_____

_____

_____

_____

Exercise: This week, be intentional about scheduling time to work on your priorities. Allocate at least 30 minutes a day to work on these priorities. That may not seem like a lot of time but when you reach the end of the week you will see how each of these 30-minute blocks has assisted you in establishing the habit of working on your priorities. This exercise is all about implementation.

Affirmation:

"I will make my goals in life a priority and not depend on others to make them a reality for me."

_____

_____

_____

_____

_____

_____

My priorities this week are:

1.

_____

_____

_____

_____

_____

_____

2.

_____

_____

_____

_____

_____

_____

3.

_____

_____

_____

_____

_____

_____

Reflection

Principle 46

Be present not busy showing you're present.

We are living in the social media age where everything (literally everything) is put on display for the world to see in our personal and professional lives. We have become consumed with having our phones out to take pictures and record videos to post and show in real time where we are, what amazing events or experiences we are a part of, and how much fun our lives are. There is absolutely nothing wrong with capturing these moments. However, the question then becomes, do we really need to post it right then and there in the moment? By doing this, we have shifted our intention and energy from being present and enjoying the moment into a space of intention to show what we are doing. If you've ever been to an unplugged concert where they make you lock your phone up in a locker or a portable pouch, you have experienced what being present in the moment truly feels like! Let's change the narrative by capturing the moment and then putting our phones away to truly enjoy the moment.

Q: What steps can you take to eliminate distractions (such as being on your phone) to create a sense and feeling of being present in the moment?

A:

_____

_____

_____

Exercise: Write down how it would feel for you to be present in the moment at an event (family gathering, concert, etc.) that you will attend or a conversation that you will have this week.

Prompt

When I am present in the moment, I will -

_____

_____

_____

_____

_____

_____

_____

_____

_____

_____

_____

_____

_____

_____

_____

_____

_____

_____

_____

Reflection

Principle 47

The ones who win are the ones who are consistent.

Winning comes from the innate ability to continue going when you encounter a loss or defeat in any given situation. The only difference between individuals who are seen as "successful" and those who may not meet those prerequisites is that successful people DON'T QUIT and are consistently consistent in their efforts to become great at what they do. When you see individuals who have achieved greatness in their lives, it is important to understand that those people achieve greatness because they're hypervigilant in cracking the code on their lives and in their craft. It may take ten years of hard work before you see your breakthrough and "success," but to get there, you must be consistent day after day. Nothing happens overnight, and it is important to understand that consistency is the key. Hard Work + Consistency = WINS

Q: Are you consistent in your efforts to be successful and win? If so, what does this look like as it relates to the principals of your work ethic in life?

A:

_____

_____

Q: If you are easily discouraged about something not working out or in the time frame you desire, what are some steps you can take to shift your mindset to create consistency in your life?

A:

_____

_____

Exercise: This week, work each day to stay consistent in everything you plan to accomplish. Keep in mind that this principle will transcend beyond the scope of this week. The goal here is to create an ecosystem in your life where you are doing the work no matter what your daily results may be.

This week I will stay consistent in the following areas of my life:

1.

_____

_____

_____

_____

_____

_____

2.

_____

_____

_____

_____

_____

3.

_____

_____

_____

_____

_____

Reflection

Principle 48

Don't downsize your vision to fit your current reality.

It can be easy to get caught up in seeing where you are and think that this is as far as you will go. The magic of visualization is seeing into the future of where you want to be. It can be a few months from now or a few years from now. However, it is important that you don't downsize your vision to fit your current reality or circumstances. To put it in perspective even further, you are always transitioning into the next level of your life. Even at this moment, as you are reading this book and working through each principle, you are setting the intention and doing the internal work to become your next upgrade in life, transitioning into becoming a better version of yourself!

Q: Where do you want to be five or ten years from now? How can you prepare your space and reality to accommodate your future self?

A:

_____

_____

_____

Q: Close your eyes and take a moment to visualize where you were five years ago in your life. Now, open your eyes and look around at your current reality. Did you see yourself where you currently are or somewhere totally different?

A:

_____

_____

_____

Exercise: Write down a visualization of where you want to be in your life 6 months, 1 year, 5 years, and 10 years from now. After you've written these down, go into further detail about how each time period will look and assist in setting up the next phase of your life's journey.

YGT! Remember, be present in the now but prepare your vision for the abundance that awaits you in the future! Have confidence and belief in the fact that your work and vision will come to pass. Patience is key. YOU GOT THIS!

6 Months   1 Year   5 Years   10 Years

_____

_____

_____

_____

_____

Plan of Action   Plan of Action   Plan of Action   Plan of Action

_____

_____

_____

_____

_____

_____

Reflection

Principle 49

Small wins accumulate to BIG WINS!

We all want the big wins in life. Trust me, WE WILL GET THEM! But first, we must understand that the small, daily wins we experience accumulate into the bigger ones. Shift your focus to work on the daily exercise of improving and achieving the small goals because these are the things that create the foundation for the big wins. Star athletes don't start out setting records in the Olympics. Their small wins likely started in grade school, one step at a time to build muscle, momentum, and speed to run and win each race. Focus on the small things, and you will win BIG!

Q: How will you stay engaged in the process of small wins on your journey to achieve the big wins?

A:

_____

_____

_____

_____

_____

_____

_____

_____

Exercise: Think about a goal that you are about to embark on. What are some aspects of achieving that goal that will require daily work and small wins? Write them down and write out the BIG wins you desire for the near future as it relates to the small wins.

Small wins this week:

1.

_____

_____

_____

2.

_____

_____

_____

3.

_____

_____

_____

4.

_____

_____

_____

5.

_____

_____

_____

Big wins I desire:

1.

_____

_____

_____

_____

2.

_____

_____

_____

_____

3.

_____

_____

_____

_____

4.

_____

_____

_____

_____

5.

_____

_____

_____

_____

Reflection

Principle 50

Don't be afraid to be YOU!

Out of all the people living on this earth, there is only one you! You were put here to be great and create an impact and legacy that will live on forever. Your gifts and talents are unique to you, just as your personality is, and you should embrace that daily. Have confidence in who you are, and you will attract people and energy that aligns with your values and vibration.

Q: What is an aspect of yourself and personality that you have been afraid to let shine through?

A:

_____

_____

_____

_____

_____

_____

Q: What steps can you take to embrace your full authentic self and show up as that person day after day from here on out?

A:

_____

_____

_____

_____

_____

_____

Exercise: Make a list of the personality traits that you are super proud of. Now, write down the ones you have feared showing to the world. Lastly, create a list of why you have been afraid to be all those things and how you can push through the fear of being your 100% true and authentic self. Reflect on this list throughout this week.

Prompt:

I am super proud of my:

_____

_____

_____

_____

_____

I have been afraid to be:

_____

_____

_____

_____

_____

I will push through my fear by:

_____

_____

_____

_____

_____

Reflection

Principle 51

Momentum creates progress.

Just as a ship sailing or a plane flying across the world, momentum in your life inevitably creates progress toward your future. Often, the hardest step to take is the first one (Principle #1: Just Start!) Whether starting a new workout routine, leaving a job to start your own business, or moving to a new city to start a new chapter of your life. The first steps can be difficult to take, and most times, the fear of the unknown on the other side of that step creates resistance. But the great part is that once you take that first step, you shift the world's energy and create momentum to continue building upon. When you start that new workout routine, you may be sore on day two, but you are making progress and building momentum to create a healthy lifestyle change (internal work) and a physically fit physique (by-product of your internal work).

Q: What is something that you've been wanting to accomplish but fear has prevented you from creating the initial momentum?

A:

_____

_____

_____

Q: Once you have the momentum, how will you continue creating positive momentum and measure your progress to keep going and stay motivated?

A:

_____

_____

_____

Exercise: Think about a time when you were making progress and creating momentum in a particular area of your life. Now fast-forward to your present reality and list some of the ways you can remain in a state of flow with your momentum and progress.

Prompt:

I will maintain my momentum by -

_____

_____

_____

_____

_____

_____

_____

_____

_____

I will measure my progress by -

_____

_____

_____

_____

_____

_____

_____

_____

Reflection

Principle 52

Getting out of your own way can be a gamechanger.

At times, we can be our own worst enemy or biggest critic and stand in our own way. When we are working to accomplish things in life, it is difficult for us to remove ourselves from the situation and see ourselves in a different light to:

1. See our progress.
2. Note the areas where we can improve.
3. See alternative methods of how we can improve.
4. Allow others to help us.

Sometimes, you just need to get out of your own way and open yourself up to be helped, constructively criticized by others who want to see us win and ASK for HELP! No one can do it all on their own and the sooner you can get out of your own way, the sooner you can take your life and accomplishments to the next level.

_____

_____

_____

_____

_____

_____

_____

Exercise: Think of a time when you know for a fact that you stood in your own way. In the future, what would you change to set yourself up for the best possible outcome of success? Write down how you will transform your narrative to get out of your own way.

I will get out of my own way by:

1.

_____

_____

_____

2.

_____

_____

_____

3.

_____

_____

_____

4.

_____

_____

_____

5.

_____

_____

_____

Reflection

Principle 53

Take it all in stride.

Everything that happens on your journey in life plays a vital role in who you are right now and who you are becoming. There will be peaks when things are going according to plan and valleys in which you will be pushed to reflect and assess things from a different perspective. No matter what, there is something to be learned from both the peaks and the valleys of life. Take it all in stride because at the end of the day, they are there to make you a stronger person.

Q: How do you handle adversity when things don't go according to plan?

A:

_____

_____

_____

_____

_____

_____

_____

_____

_____

_____

_____

_____

Exercise: Keep a positive mindset in every situation that happens in your life. Some moments may be easier than others but work to find the good in every situation. Repeat the following affirmation when difficult and challenging moments happen this week and beyond.

Affirmation: "I will remain positive and steadfast on my journey in life to take all things in stride while becoming the greatest version of myself."

_____

_____

_____

_____

_____

_____

_____

_____

_____

_____

_____

_____

_____

_____

_____

_____

_____

_____

Reflection

Principle 54

Comparison is the killer of joy.

Have you ever looked at someone else's life and said, "I wish that was me?" Yes, we have all said this at one time or another. When those moments happen, we immediately feel a sense of lack or disappointment because we have subconsciously compared ourselves to another person's life. Comparison is the biggest killer of joy. You must take inventory of your life and realize that everyone's journey, process, experiences in life, and blessings are different. Take a moment to look at your life and realize how blessed you are to be where you are. You may not be exactly where you want to be, but you are much closer than you once were. Remember, someone out there wishes they had half the blessings you have. You are unique and already blessed beyond measure.

Q: When is a moment in your life that you compared yourself to someone else? How did it make you feel and how did you move past that emotion?

A:

_____

_____

_____

_____

_____

Q: How do you experience joy in your life?

A:

_____

_____

_____

_____

_____

Exercise: Take a few minutes to reflect on your life thus far and write down 5 things that you are thankful for and that bring true joy to your life this week.

I am thankful for:

1.

_____

_____

_____

2.

_____

_____

_____

3.

_____

_____

_____

4.

_____

_____

_____

5.

_____

_____

_____

Reflection

Principle 55

See your vision, believe it, and realize it.

For us to accumulate the support of others, we must first be willing to give our all to our dreams and visions. No one will ever give more to your dreams than you will, and that is a fact. For your vision to come to fruition, you must have complete and utter confidence in your abilities to make your dreams a reality. Remember that your goals and dreams will come to fruition as long as you keep believing and working at them.

Q: Do you believe 100% in your vision and dream?

A:

_____

_____

_____

_____

Q: What have you done to show the world you are serious about your goals?

A:

_____

_____

_____

_____

Exercise: Write down 3 ways that you can build "Belief Equity" for your goals so that others see the value in investing in it.

My belief Equity List:

1.

_____

_____

_____

_____

_____

2.

_____

_____

_____

_____

_____

3.

_____

_____

_____

_____

_____

Reflection

Principle 56

Focus on the long game.

Life is a marathon, not a sprint. Your work today is a building block for what is to come. As mentioned in Principle 53, small wins accumulate to BIG WINS. It is key to focus on daily wins and accomplishments on a micro-scale to create success in the long term. When a seed is planted, it doesn't sprout the very next day. It takes time for the seed to establish itself underground and find its way. Eventually, the work done beneath the surface will break through to the world. The same applies to your life. Do the hard work beneath the surface and watch it flourish in the world when the time is right!

Q: Are you currently focused on the long game? If not, what needs to change with your mindset to focus on long-term success?

A:

_____

_____

_____

_____

_____

_____

_____

_____

Exercise: Write down one of your long-term goals. Now that you've written that down, think about all the steps that it will take to accomplish that goal and how you will stay consistent over the long-term to accomplish said goal. Also, write down how you will mentally prepare and approach being on this long-term journey to stay engaged.

My long-term goal is to:

_____

_____

_____

_____

_____

I will stay engaged in this long-term process by:

1.

_____

_____

_____

2.

_____

_____

_____

3.

_____

_____

_____

I will mentally prepare to accomplish my long-term goal by:

1.

_____

_____

_____

_____

_____

_____

_____

2.

_____

_____

_____

_____

_____

_____

_____

3.

_____

_____

_____

_____

_____

_____

Reflection

Back Cover Blurb

We all desire to be the best version of ourselves and improve our lives. However, we often bite off more than we can chew when it comes to creating long-lasting change in our lives for the better, and even the areas of life that we are too fearful to acknowledge exist. Often, the very thing we run from is the one thing that will drastically change our lives. The Power to WIN dives into 56 principles and aspects of life that we all deal with daily while also providing insight, reflective questions, and exercises to help you drastically improve areas of your life one day, week, and year at a time. Through using The Power to WIN, you will take full control of your life as it presently is while simultaneously building helpful skills and mindset shifts to create your true, authentic dream life. The Power to WIN will take you on a journey one principle at a time to create positive, long-lasting internal change that will totally transform how you show up in the world.

About the author

Trenton "T-Ray" Thomas is a renowned violinist, music producer, educator, entrepreneur, and empowerment speaker who embodies the term "Dreams2Reality" to build his dream life. As someone who took the "leap of faith" in 2014 by transitioning from being a full-time music teacher to working as a full-time performing artist, he has used his musical journey and self-development as a medium to empower others to chase their dream life relentlessly no matter where people are in life.

"We all have something to offer and contribute to the world in the short time we are here, and it is important to help others find their purpose and embrace their true power along the way."

-Trenton "T-Ray" Thomas